Welcome

Fellow Parents and Guardian Angels,
Thank You For Your Purchase!

D1716534

Allow me to introduce myself, my name is Orite Levy, owner and curator/designer of,
Assorted Arts Press Kids!.
&
Assorted Arts Press
.

Not only am I a strong small business owner but a proud single mother of
a growing son and full time caretaker for my 93yo gran.
As you can see, family is important to me and so are our children.
It is my goal to make quality books for all kids and as a parent who has homeschooled for
years, i feel I have a handle on what works well and is worth while, however,
I would LOVE your feedback.

If you love this book, by all means show it with a great review...

GIVE ME YOUR THOUGHTS!

I am in need of reviews to boost this budding business, however
if you have anything other than a five star review, feel free to leave it if you feel the need
and also, I would ask for your personal feedback instead as poor reviews are damaging..
Please contact me letting me know what YOU would
change to make this book even better.
Or, tell me what it is that you think needs adjusting. I am open to
YOUR outside perspective and welcome it!
Let me hear your voices!

Happily raving reviews also welcome... ☺
It takes a community and I am glad to have you as a part of ours.

Direct all comments to Assortedartspress@gmail.com
Include the book you are referencing.
Thanks!

Please check out all our other books by scanning the QR code on the following page

Student Information:

Year: ....

Age: ....

Grade: ....

For all of our other
books scan the QR
code below

SCAN
ME

If you and your child like and enjoy this book, please leave a good review. Include pictures of your child's work as it helps other parents find great tools like this one for their kids and helps our company to flourish and continue producing great quality designs for children everywhere.

From our hearts to yours, we Thank You!

Book At A Glance

- Creates and forms the base of a gratitude mindset.

- Boosts self esteem and confidence

- Introduces simple examples of gratitude which help shift the child's greater perspective of personal abundance.

- Initiates healthy self talk perspectives.

- Helps to direct the mind away from negative perspectives that may over time, develop into more negative mental states.

- Raises the level of consciousness in the child.

- Helps build a foundation of gratitude, or a "Grateful Nature".

- Builds a lifelong structure for a positive mindset in all things.

Bringing it back to simple: Although this book may seem super simple, that is the point. Making gratitude fun and basic allows your children to easily adapt this practice into their lives. The flow of creativity may even spark a life long appreciation of the little things that make up our larger lives. It all counts and needs all be counted.

In a world where we are predisposed to depression and other, our children need us to show them how to direct their minds in order to achieve high level mental health, success and wellbeing. These practices are life changing and are one tool in many, that will boost your child's success in this ever changing world. We provide the foundation, let's provide a solid one. ☺

Daily Affirmations

Though this workbook is dedicated to "Gratitude Practice", it is also very important to begin practices of positive affirmations as well. Repeat these affirmations daily along with your gratitudes and when ready, move on to our "I AM Positive Affirmations Handwriting Practice Books"

Not only will your child learn to start a positive affirmation practice but they will also improve their handwriting skills at the same time.

For now, repeat the following affirmations with your young child daily.

Say These With Conviction and Zest for Life!

I choose to be happy. I AM happy!

I believe in myself. I AM awesome!

I always do my best.

I AM creative

I CAN do it!

I AM courageous.

I AM kind to myself and others always.

I feel amazing.

I have everything I need for success within me.

I can change easily and appreciate growth.

I am in charge of how I feel at all times.

People love and adore me always.

I love myself

I am successful in everything I do.

I take action daily toward my success.

I learn easily and try new things often.

I AM a leader, I know "failures" are my biggest lessons.

I learn from my mistakes and go back to life stronger and smarter.

I have a success mindset.

Life and change are exciting to me.

I am fearless.

I know I am worthy. I AM worthy.

I AM strong and know I will succeed in reaching my dreams.

I persist in reaching my goals.

A note to the Adults:

Hello fellow Adults,

Thank you for choosing this book for your growing young minds.
By choosing this book you are setting your children up for success.
This simplistic way of teaching gratitude will last a lifetime especially when taught young.

Gratitude practice is at the core of every very successful human, and teaching this practice consistently from a young age, will help substantially in the emotional growth and development of the student in the years to come. We call this front loading emotional health and wellness.

Learning to find gratitude for all the tiny things in life helps provide a much larger perspective to all who practice. Remembering daily all that we have already in our lives to be thankful for, helps us to stay present in an over stimulating world. Remembering and stating our gratitudes for the smaller things does two things, first, it helps us stay grounded in recognizing that we already have so much more than many and that we are super fortunate, wether it be that we have shoes and someone else does not etc... ALL the little things matter. The other thing that this practice provides, is a mindset that is geared toward abundance and not lack. Recognizing all that we have on a daily basis will allow one to feel fulfilled and not wanting all the time. This state of being can create and allow for more abundance and general flow in life. ie, Less Stress!

Another important impression to make is that practice is what gets us to our goals and taking daily action, such as practicing gratitude, tracing/writing & drawing daily will create an outcome, in this case, it is a deeper connection to the child's personal abundance, much better penmanship and finer artwork. All cases differ depending on what is being practiced. This style of daily action is setting kids up for successful life habits, for balance and for good mental wellbeing.

Thank you for your support and for supporting young minds!

For The Kids!

Some questions to ponder and answer...
(with adult assistance: adults, really discuss gratitude on all levels)

How can we show our gratitude?

What does "Gratitude" mean to you?

What is a "Gratitude Practice"?

What does gratitude do for us?

How does it feel to be grateful?

Why is it important to be and stay grateful?

Why is making gratitude an everyday practice important?

GRATITUDE

ATTITUDE

A note to the kids about gratitude and practicing it...

Definition: Grateful - Feeling or showing an appreciation of kindness; deeply thankful. Feels like a heart full of love. ♡ In this case, deeply thankful for all that one has, experiences, or is.

Gratitude is more of a feeling than anything. It is that feeling you get in your heart when you are happy. You know the one.
Think of how it feels to get something you have been looking forward to, or when you get a surprise.
≷♡≷ That joy. ≷♡≷
Remember it?

While you are practicing gratitude or any positive affirmations, it is very important to feel and recreate that feeling of happiness in your body, the one that you have in your heart when you feel really happy or joyous.
Do your best to consciously create that feeling in your body as you do your gratitude and affirmation activities and understand also that all that you have, some others do not, this helps you to very importantly remain conscious of how fortunate you really are, no matter what.
One pointer, if you think of how you would feel if you didn't have all the things in this book, you will understand what it is to feel and be grateful for what you do have on an even deeper level.
Remember to cherish your abundance and show it with a great "Gratitude Practice"!
Your practice will soon become your nature and a grateful nature can lead you to lifelong success and happiness. Cherish yourself and your life, as you, are amazing.
♥˅♥˅♥˅♥

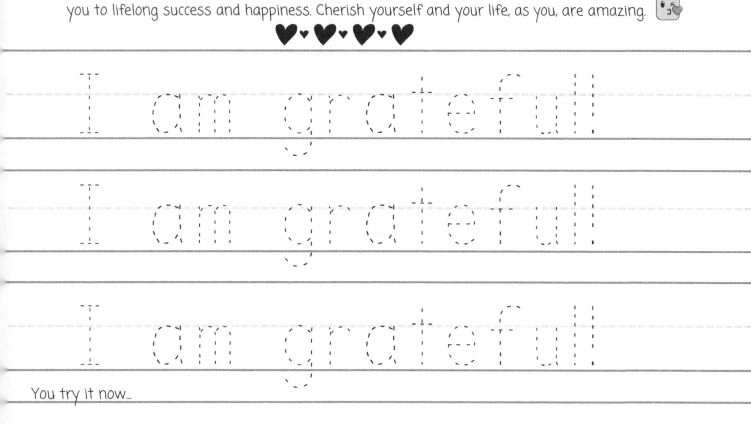

You try it now...

Draw your bed..

I AM GRATEFUL FOR...

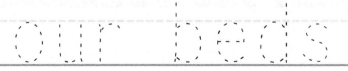

You try it now...

Draw a book

I AM GRATEFUL FOR...

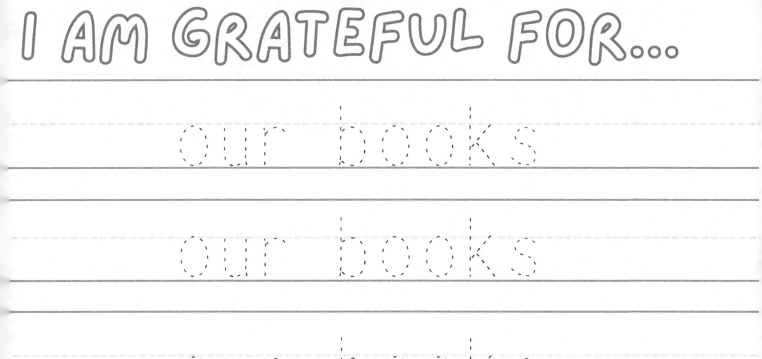

our books

our books

our books

ou try it now...

Draw your toys.

I AM GRATEFUL FOR...

our toys

our toys

our toys

You try it now...

Draw your home.

I AM GRATEFUL FOR...

our home

our home

our home

You try it now...

Draw your car..

I AM GRATEFUL FOR...

our car

our car

our car

You try it now...

Draw your shoes.

I AM GRATEFUL FOR...

my shoes

my shoes

my shoes

ou try it now...

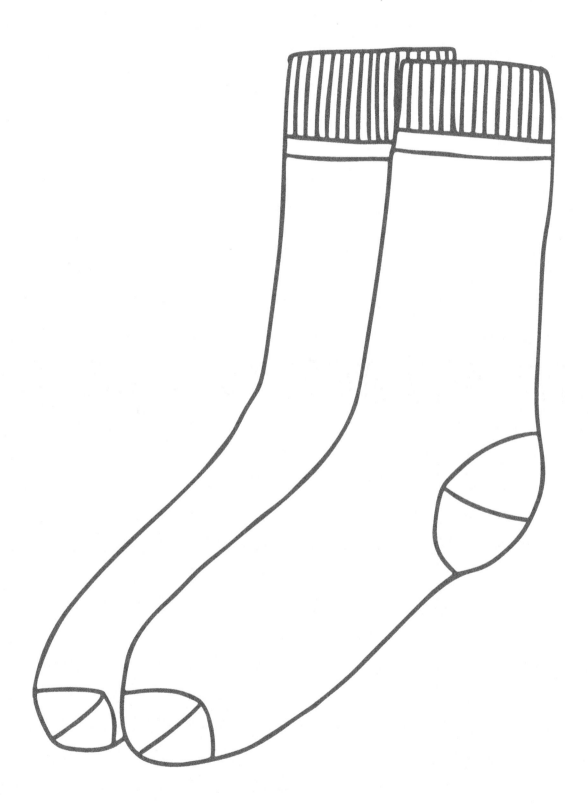

Draw your socks.

I AM GRATEFUL FOR...

my socks

my socks

my socks

You try it now...

Draw your shirt.

I AM GRATEFUL FOR...

my shirts

my shirts

my shirts

ou try it now...

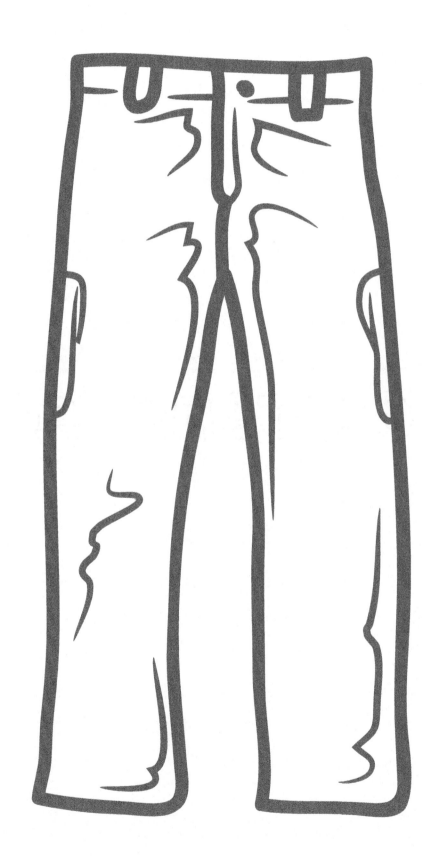

Draw your pants.

I AM GRATEFUL FOR...

my pants

my pants

my pants

You try it now...

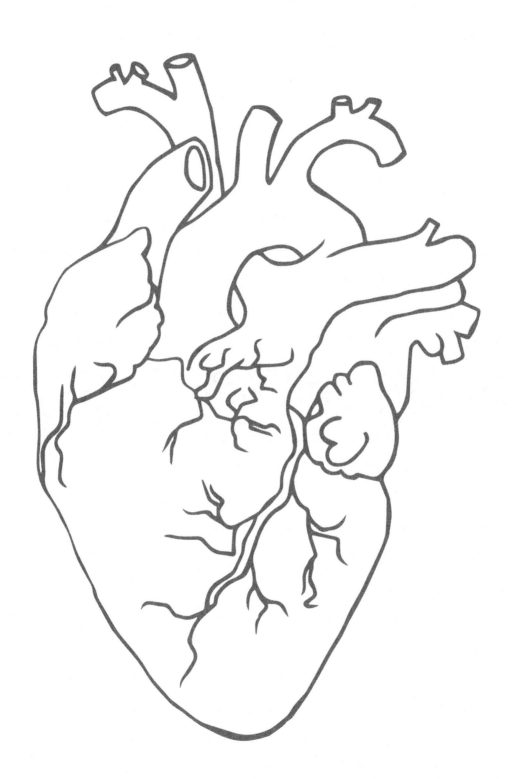

Draw your heart.

I AM GRATEFUL FOR...

my heart

my heart

my heart

you try it now...

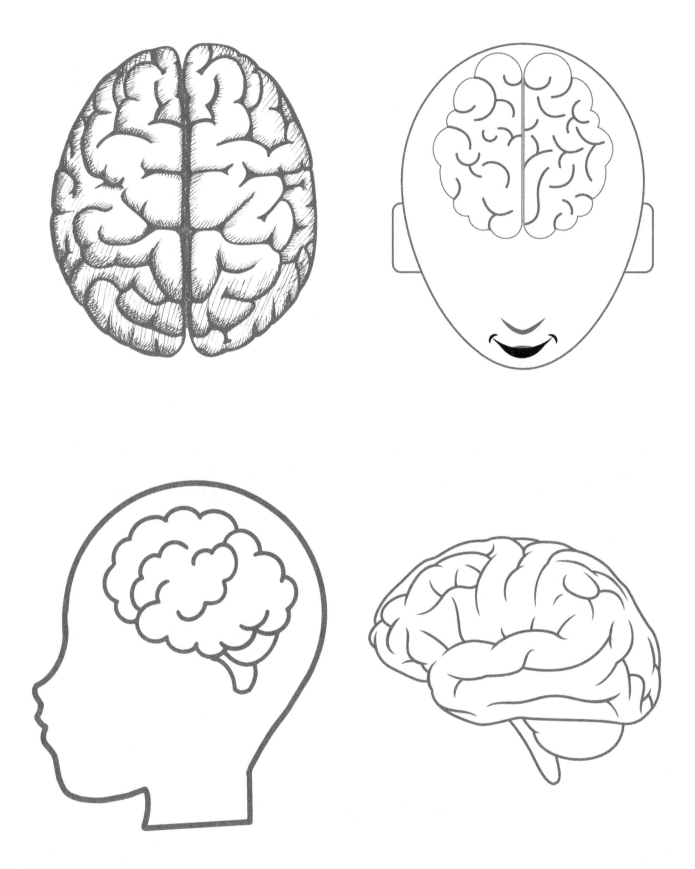

Draw your brain.

I AM GRATEFUL FOR...

my brain

my brain

my brain

You try it now...

Draw your nose.

I AM GRATEFUL FOR...

my nose

my nose

my nose

ou try it now...

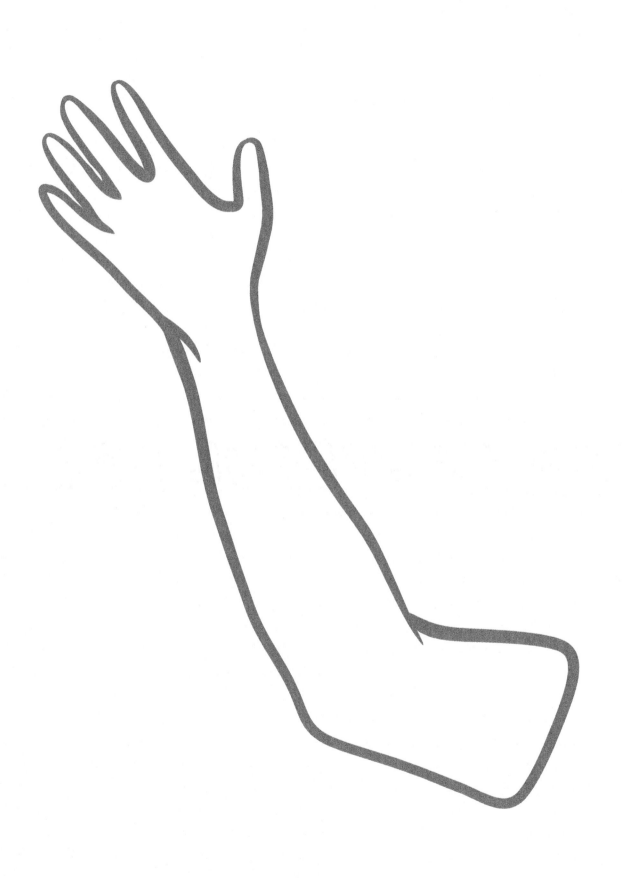

Draw your arms.

I AM GRATEFUL FOR...

my arms

my arms

my arms

You try it now...

Draw your smile.

I AM GRATEFUL FOR...

my smile

my smile

my smile

You try it now...

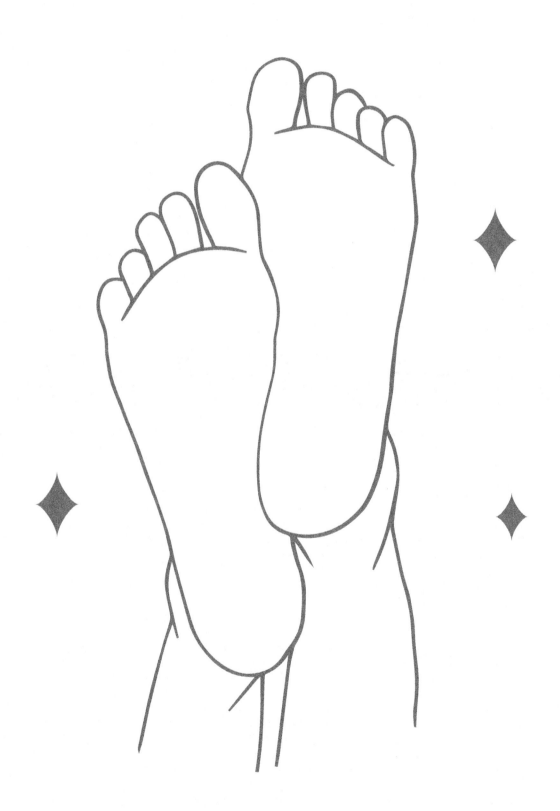

Draw your feet..

I AM GRATEFUL FOR...

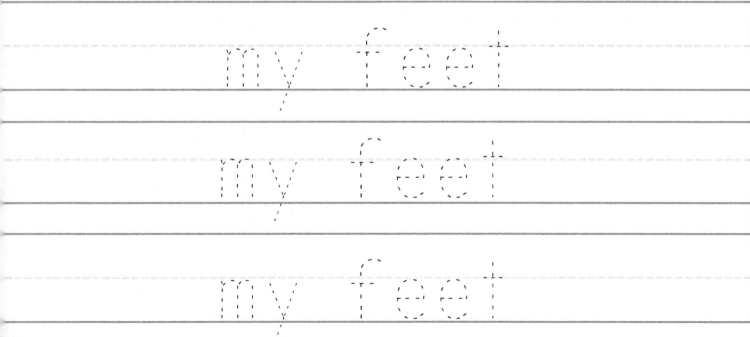

You try it now...

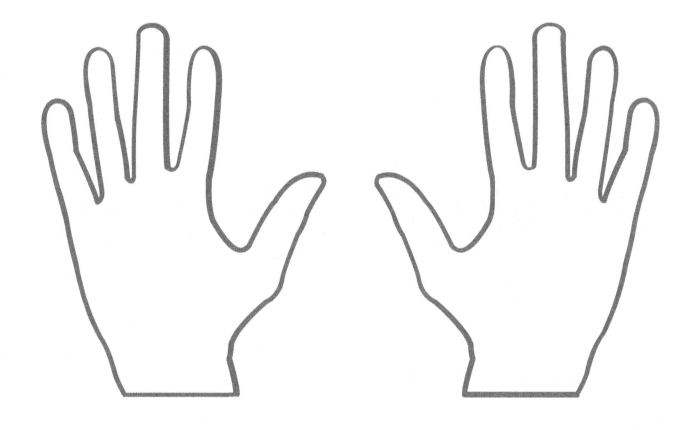

Draw your hands.

I AM GRATEFUL FOR...

my hands

my hands

my hands

you try it now...

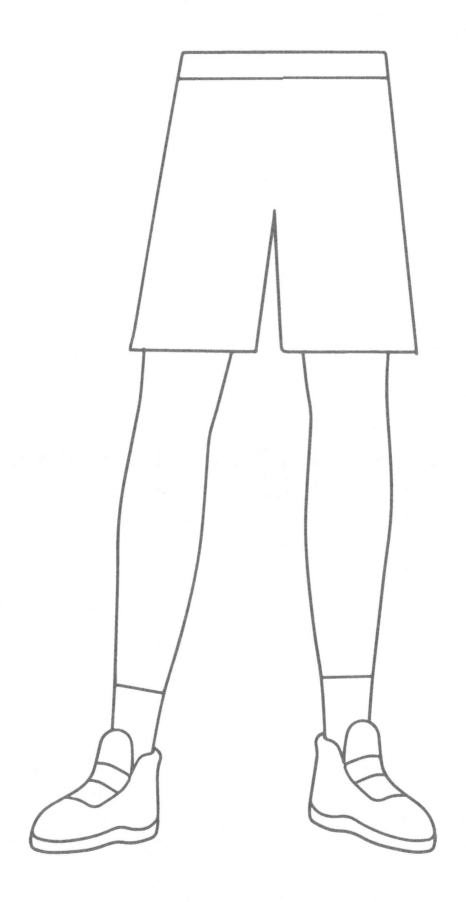

Draw your legs.

I AM GRATEFUL FOR...

my legs

my legs

my legs

You try it now...

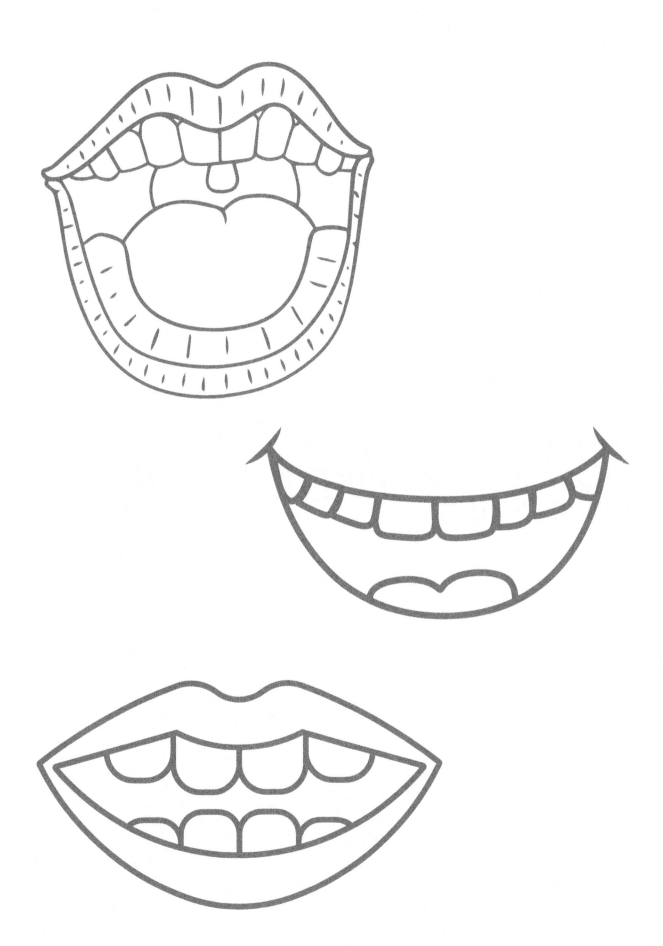

Draw your mouth.

I AM GRATEFUL FOR...

my mouth

my mouth

my mouth

you try it now...

Draw your eyes.

I AM GRATEFUL FOR...

my eyes

my eyes

my eyes

You try it now...

ears

Draw your ears.

I AM GRATEFUL FOR...

my ears

my ears

my ears

ou try it now...

Draw your teeth.

I AM GRATEFUL FOR...

my teeth

my teeth

my teeth

You try it now...

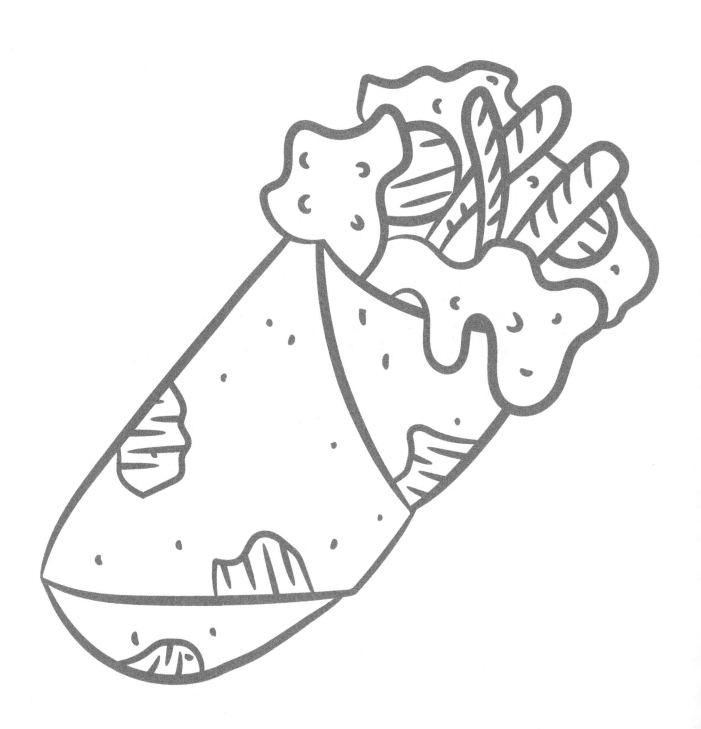

Draw your food.

I AM GRATEFUL FOR...

food

food

food

ou try it now...

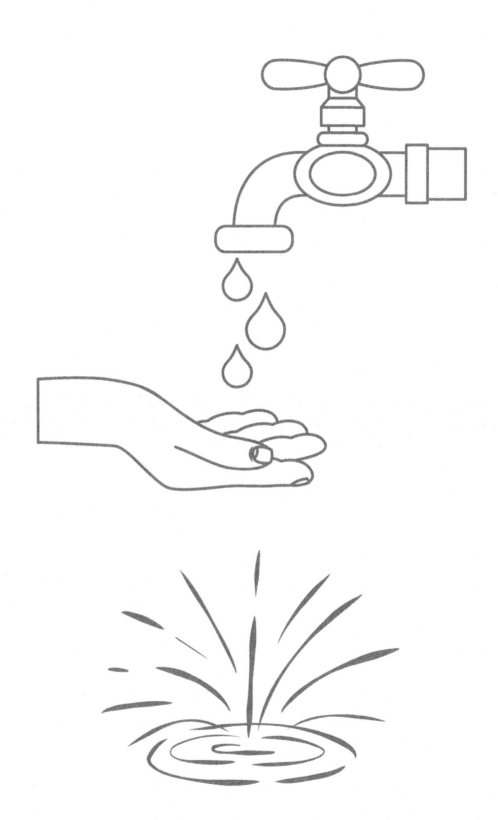

Draw water.

I AM GRATEFUL FOR...

water

water

water

You try it now...

All families are unique and special in their own way!
Celebrate your uniqueness and accept
other families special
uniqueness
too!

Draw your family.

I AM GRATEFUL FOR...

family

family

family

ou try it now...

Draw a kid...

I AM GRATEFUL FOR...

kids

kids

kids

You try it now...

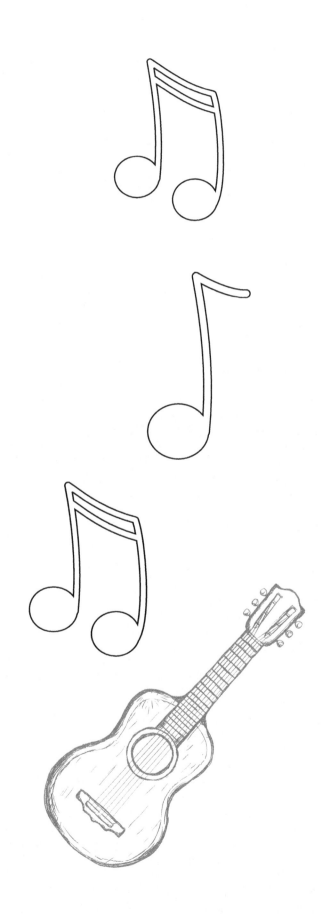

Draw something musical.

I AM GRATEFUL FOR...

music

music

music

ou try it now...

Draw yourself dancing.

I AM GRATEFUL FOR...

dancing

dancing

dancing

You try it now...

Draw a bird.

I AM GRATEFUL FOR...

birds

birds

birds

ou try it now...

Draw a bee.

I AM GRATEFUL FOR...

You try it now...

Draw a bug.

I AM GRATEFUL FOR...

bugs

bugs

bugs

you try it now...

Draw a frog.

I AM GRATEFUL FOR...

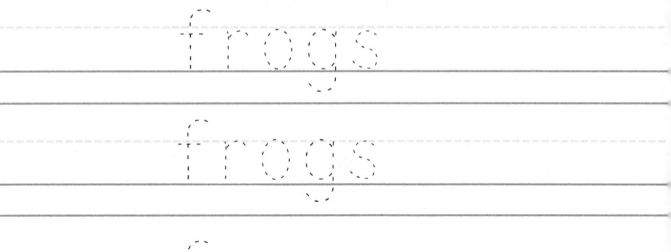

You try it now...

Draw a dog.

I AM GRATEFUL FOR...

dogs

dogs

dogs

you try it now...

Draw a cat.

I AM GRATEFUL FOR...

cats

cats

cats

You try it now...

Draw a tree.

I AM GRATEFUL FOR...

trees

trees

trees

Draw snow.

○

I AM GRATEFUL FOR...

the snow

the snow

the snow

You try it now...

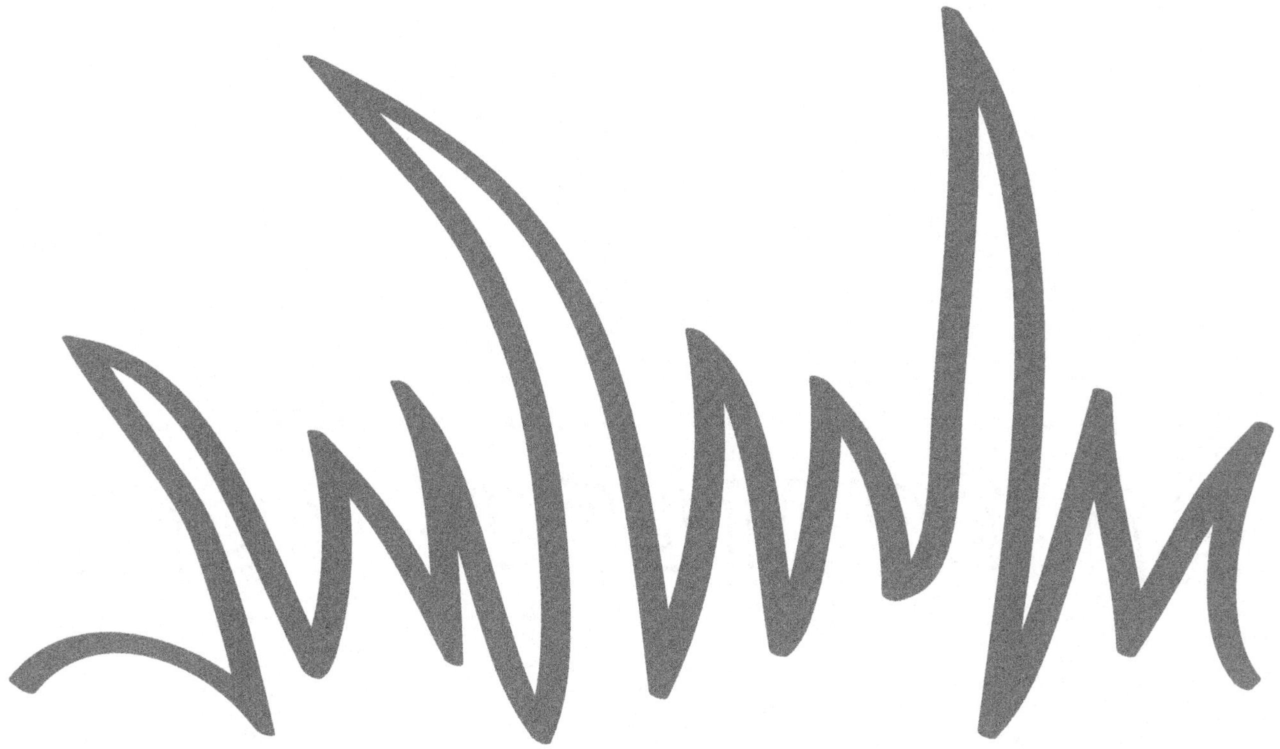

Draw grass.

I AM GRATEFUL FOR...

grass

grass

grass

ou try it now...

Draw leaves.

I AM GRATEFUL FOR...

leaves

leaves

leaves

You try it now...

Draw rain falling.

I AM GRATEFUL FOR...

the rain

the rain

the rain

you try it now...

Draw the ocean.

I AM GRATEFUL FOR...

the oceans

the oceans

the oceans

You try it now...

Draw the stars.

I AM GRATEFUL FOR...

the stars

the stars

the stars

ou try it now...

Draw the sun.

I AM GRATEFUL FOR...

the sun

the sun

the sun

ou try it now...

Draw the moon.

I AM GRATEFUL FOR...

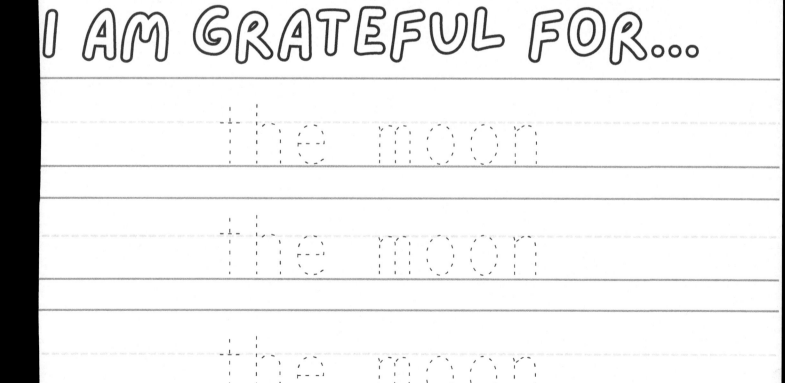

the moon

the moon

the moon

try it now...

Draw the earth.

I AM GRATEFUL FOR...

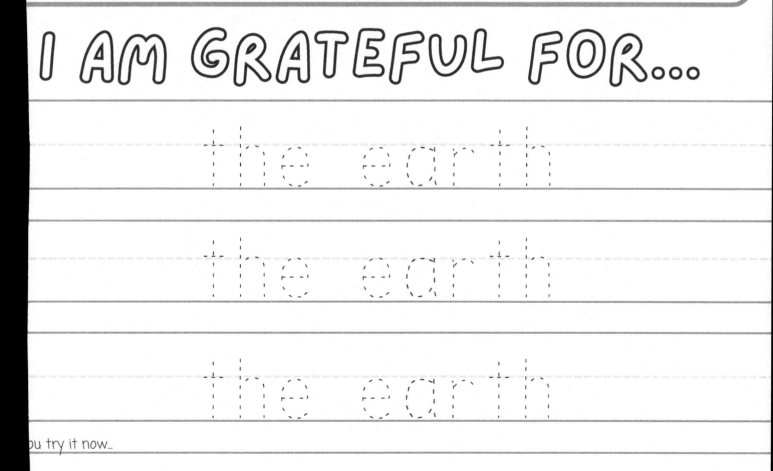

the earth

the earth

the earth

ou try it now...

Draw your favorite thing about your life.

I AM GRATEFUL FOR...

my life

my life

my life

try it now...

All Assorted Arts Press Coloring Books & Assorted Arts Press Kids! Educational Workbooks
are curated by compiling various assorted artist's art and combining them, to make
creative, fun pages to look at, write on and color, showing that many different styles of art,
can beautifully flow together to create many enjoyable books
and moments of creative coloring, writing and drawing inspiration.
If you would like to be notified of new releases and general news, please email us
AssortedArtsPress@gmail.com
Subject: "Updates"

Made in the USA
Monee, IL
12 October 2022